DATE DUE

4/26	5B	1-23	6N
5/11	5C	2/12	5B
9/2	5B	2/22	6N
9/9	5C	3/6	6N
9/23/99	5B		
11-18	5B		
12/1	4S		
1-14-00	3Y		
2/1	4S		
3/9	5C		
3/20	3Y		
4/25	4S		
5/9	4S		
9/21	2K		
10/18	5C		
12/12	6A		

Inside the NBA

Los Angeles Lakers

Paul Joseph

ABDO & Daughters
PUBLISHING

Published by Abdo & Daughters, 4940 Viking Dr., Suite 622, Edina, MN 55435.

Copyright ©1997 by Abdo Consulting Group, Inc., Pentagon Tower, P.O. Box 36036, Minneapolis, Minnesota 55435. International copyrights reserved in all countries. No part of this book may be reproduced in any form without written permission from the publisher. Printed in the United States.

Cover photo: Allsport
Interior photos: Allsport, pages 1, 5, 17, 21, 22, 27
Wide World Photos, pages 7, 9, 10, 14, 28

Edited by Kal Gronvall

Library of Congress Cataloging–in–Publication Data

Joseph, Paul, 1970-
  The Los Angeles Lakers / by Paul Joseph
    p. cm. — (Inside the NBA)
  Includes index.
  Summary: Provides an overview of the history and key personalities connected with the team whose winning seasons have featured such players as George Mikan, Magic Johnson, Jerry West, Wilt Chamberlain, and Kareem Abdul-Jabbar.
  ISBN 1-56239-762-1
  1. Los Angeles Lakers (Basketball team)—Juvenile literature.
[1. Los Angeles Lakers (Basketball team)—History. 2. Basketball—History.] I. Title. II. Series.
GV885.52.L67J67 1997
796.323' 64' 0979494—dc21   96-39616
                                                              CIP
                                                              AC

Contents

Los Angeles Lakers

Since 1960, the Los Angeles Lakers have resided in sunny southern California. The Lakers, however, got their name from their original home, Minneapolis, Minnesota. The state of Minnesota is known for its 10,000 lakes.

Whether the Lakers played in Minneapolis or Los Angeles, they always dominated. In the 1940s and 1950s in Minneapolis, they won with the first basketball superstar, George Mikan. In the 1980s in Los Angeles, they won five National Basketball Association (NBA) championships with one of the greatest players of all time: Magic Johnson.

Between those times, they had outstanding All-Stars like Elgin Baylor, Jerry West, Wilt Chamberlain, and Kareem Abdul-Jabbar. Although the Lakers only won one NBA title during this time, they still managed to dominate the Western Conference, winning it a whopping seven times in the 1960s. The Lakers seemed to always be overshadowed by the Boston Celtics. But the fact is the Lakers have won an incredible 11 NBA Championships, and in the 1980s they had the upper hand over the Celtics.

Recently, the Lakers have been known as Magic's team. Today, they are known as Shaquille O'Neal's team. And in the very beginning, the Lakers were known as Mikan's team.

Facing page: The Lakers' Shaquille O'Neal.

George Mikan

George Mikan was the NBA's first superstar and probably did more to popularize professional basketball than any other player in the history of the game. Mikan was an accurate shooter with dazzling playmaking skills.

The 6-foot, 10-inch bespectacled Mikan changed the way centers played the game. Before Mikan, centers were defensive specialists, content to cover the basket and bat away shots. Mikan was the first big man to develop a hook shot and pass with precision.

The Minneapolis Lakers joined the NBA in 1948 after playing in two other leagues. Mikan had already won three championships in the other two leagues, but it was in the NBA where he and the Lakers began to take off.

The Lakers, behind George Mikan, won their first-ever NBA title in the 1948-49 season. Minneapolis took the best-of-seven series in six games, including a 40-point performance from Mikan in the final game.

The Lakers were by no means a one-man show. Although Mikan was the star he did have a great supporting cast. Jim Pollard was a "can't miss" shooting forward, six-foot, seven-inch Verne Mikkelsen was a hard-playing rebound specialist, and Slater "Dugie" Martin was the slick-passing point guard.

The Lakers had such an all-around awesome lineup that in the first All-Star Game in 1951, Minneapolis had four starters on the Western team.

Minneapolis followed up their championship season with another title in 1950. But in 1951, when they sent four starters to the All-Star Game, the Lakers were upset in the playoffs. They came back the following three years with a vengeance, even after the NBA changed the rules to slow Mikan down.

Minneapolis Lakers' center George Mikan breaks up a shot by Rochester Royals' guard Bob Davies.

First Dynasty

The rest of the teams in the NBA wondered what to do about Mikan. He was dominating the league and was nearly impossible to defend. After the 1951 season the league made some rule changes to try to slow Mikan down. The biggest rule change was widening the lane from 6 to 12 feet so Mikan couldn't be as close to the basket for long periods of time.

But the rules did little to stop Mikan. He still led the league in scoring with a 24-point average, including a career-high 61-point game. More important, he led his team back to the 1952 NBA Finals, where the team defeated the New York Knicks in seven games.

The NBA tried to slow Mikan down, but it didn't work. He proved again how dominant he was as he led the Lakers back to the NBA Finals in 1953. Once again the Lakers faced the Knicks. Although all of the games were close, the Lakers prevailed in five games to win their second title in a row.

In 1954, Mikan was often injured and his bad knees were slowing him down. But he still had enough in him to have the league's fourth-best scoring average and lead the league in rebounds with 17 per game. Behind Mikan, Minneapolis beat the Syracuse Nationals in seven games. It was the Lakers' third NBA championship in a row and their fifth in six years. But the championship days were over for Minnesota NBA fans. After winning his fifth NBA title, George Mikan announced his retirement at age 29.

Mikan's name may not be very familiar to young basketball fans, but he was the first big star in the NBA. He changed the style of the game by combining size with athleticism. Without him there might not be a National Basketball Association. One thing is for sure. Without Mikan the Lakers never would have had their first dynasty.

Elgin Baylor fights for two points down low against the Boston Celtics.

The New Laker Star

The Minneapolis Lakers were in serious trouble after George Mikan retired. Mikan stayed on with the organization as general manager but in no way could he do from the front office what he had done on the court.

By 1957, the Lakers were a losing team and were not attracting fans to the games. In an effort to boost the team Mikan was named head coach. After a start of 9 wins and 30 losses Mikan was back upstairs in the front office.

After finishing the year with only 19 wins, the Lakers got the first pick in the college draft. In 1958, the Lakers introduced their newest star, Elgin Baylor, to the basketball world. The six-foot, five-inch, 225-pound forward brought a new individual brand of basketball to the league.

Baylor was the first player known for such tricks as changing directions in midair and sinking impossible off-balance shots. Later Julius Erving and Michael Jordan would demonstrate the same moves that Baylor had used.

Baylor was also an exceptional rebounder who followed up his missed shots by scoring tap-ins. Elgin was not only a fan-favorite in Minneapolis but also throughout the country. He became the star attraction in the NBA with sell-outs being the norm at stadiums at which he played.

In Baylor's rookie season he was fourth in scoring with 24.9 points per game, third in rebounds, and second in minutes played. For his play he was named NBA Rookie of the Year. Thanks to him, the Lakers made it to the NBA Finals. Although the Celtics swept the Lakers in four straight, they were back on track.

The Lakers may have been back on track, but the team was having financial difficulties. The NBA was a hard sell in Minnesota, so to keep the franchise afloat they decided they needed to leave the Lake Country and head for the ocean.

Jerry West drives the lane for an uncontested layup against the Cincinnati Royals.

Lakers Get
And Go West

The Lakers got a new home in 1960. They moved west and set up shop in Los Angeles. Along with moving west they drafted West—Jerry West, that is. West would become the newest star in the NBA. At 6-foot, 3-inches, 175 pounds, West was one of the best shooters in basketball.

With Baylor and West, the Lakers had the best two-man team in the league. The two played beautifully together. They shared top billing unselfishly, and as a result they led their team to the Finals year after year.

The two stars were not enough to boost attendance. The average home game was played in front of fewer than 4,000 filled seats. Playoff games struggled to sell 5,000 seats. And all this despite record-setting games by their stars. Baylor set a single-game record for scoring with 71 points. And West scored 63 points in one game—a record for guards. Both players set these records with less than 3,000 fans watching the game in the arena.

With the ownership debating whether to fold the franchise, the Lakers made it to their first Finals in Los Angeles in 1962. The fans began to respond with sky-rocketing attendance. The Lakers knew then that they had found a permanent place to call home.

The 1960s: Great Teams, No Titles

During the 1960s, the Lakers were to come so close, so often, and be beaten so regularly by the same team—the dreaded Boston Celtics—that it was maddening. For Elgin Baylor and Jerry West it became a public agony.

In the 1962 NBA Finals the series went back and forth. The first four games were tight all the way, and any team could have won. In Game 5, with the series tied at two games apiece, Baylor took over with 61 points to lead the Lakers to victory. The Celtics bounced back in Game 6 to tie the series. Game 7 went to an exciting overtime, with the Celtics pulling away in the last seconds for the championship.

Even with the Finals loss, the Lakers made money, and along with the Celtics became a permanent fixture on television throughout America's living rooms.

They bounced back in 1963 to reach the NBA Finals, but like a recurring nightmare, they were eliminated by the Celtics in six.

The 1963-1964 season was an off-year for the Lakers. Their two stars were injured most of the year and the team was ousted in the playoffs in the first round.

The Lakers rebounded to make it to the 1965 Finals. Behind the play of West, who averaged 31 points per game, Baylor, who turned in 27, and the new rookie Walt Hazzard, many thought they could take the Celtics.

Unfortunately, in the Western Conference playoffs Baylor tore his left kneecap and was out, and West broke his nose. West, however, continued to play and averaged well over 40 points to give the Lakers a shot at the Celtics. But West was hurting both physically and mentally, making it an easy five game series win for the Celtics.

In 1965, the Lakers were sold to Jack Kent Cooke for five million dollars. Cooke spent another 16 million dollars building the Great Western Forum, the Lakers' present home.

With new ownership, the Lakers continued to dominate the Western Conference, making it to their fourth NBA Finals in five years against the Celtics. Again the Lakers fought hard to the finish, but in the end the Celtics prevailed in seven exciting games.

The following year the Lakers had injuries and a losing record. They were ousted in the playoffs as were the Celtics. But the next season in the 1968 Finals both teams were back for a rematch. After four games the series was tied. Then in Game 5, West sprained his ankle and the Lakers were done.

Wilt Chamberlain

Something had to be done, and Cooke did it. He traded three players, plus $250,000 for the 7-foot, 1-inch Wilt Chamberlain. If this powerful center couldn't get the team a title, who could?

The Lakers now had the three best players in the NBA. The Lakers were a shoe-in to reach the Finals and clearly the favorites for their first championship in Los Angeles.

The Lakers had the highest attendance and finished the season 55-27, with Chamberlain averaging 20 points and 21 rebounds per game.

Although Chamberlain was playing great, his teammates didn't like his selfish play, especially team leaders Baylor and West. But that didn't stop the team from reaching the Finals.

For once the Celtics were the underdogs, but the series was as even as it could get. Game 1 was a 120-118 Laker victory with West pouring in 53 points. In Game 2, Baylor rallied his team in the last minutes, scoring the final 12 points for a 2-0 series lead.

Left: Wilt Chamberlain gets by an opponent to score.

But the Celtics came back in Boston, picking up two games to even the series. The next two games were split, setting up a seventh and final game.

With Jack Kent Cooke so sure of a victory in the Forum that he had thousands of balloons in the rafters ready to come down, the Celtics came out and played hard. It went all the way down to the last seconds as the Celtics won 108-106 to steal the title. For the Lakers the nightmare continued.

The Lakers again dominated the West and made it to the 1970 Finals. This time though, there were no Celtics. Maybe the nightmare was over.

The Lakers took on the New York Knicks, who were led by Willis Reed, Walt Frazier, and Bill Bradley. After two games the series was tied. In Game 3, the Knicks won in overtime. Game's 4 and 5 were split. And in Game 6, Chamberlain poured in 45 points for a Laker victory.

Again it came down to a seventh and final game. But it happened—the same nightmare with a different team. The Knicks cruised to a 113-99 victory and the Los Angeles Lakers still looked for that elusive NBA championship.

The following year Baylor was out for the season with a torn Achilles tendon, and West missed the playoffs with a torn knee. The Lakers were easily ousted in the playoffs.

Finally A Championship!

The Lakers made a coaching change for the 1971-72 season to see if that would bring them the Championship. Bill Sharman, a former Celtic guard, took over the duties. Sharman, a tough and thorough coach who stressed conditioning, practice, and meetings, was ready for the challenge.

Sharman would have to do it without Elgin Baylor, whose knees forced him to retire. Sharman stressed team play and appointed Chamberlain the captain of the team, which worked.

The team was well balanced with Chamberlain grabbing 19.2 rebounds per game, and Happy Hairston picking up 13.1 rebounds. The scorers were, of course, West with 26 points per game, and Gail Goodrich chipping in 25.

The Lakers had a 33-game winning streak, the longest in NBA history. They coasted to the NBA Finals with a 69-13 record, the best in the history of the game to this point.

The Lakers met the Knicks again in the Finals. The Knicks were a great outside shooting team, but in no way could they match the Lakers in defense, strength, or height. But many thought the nightmare was starting again. In Game 1, in Los Angeles, the Knicks upset the Lakers.

The Lakers bounced back and won three in a row. With a three-to-one lead the Lakers looked in command and showed it in Game 5. Four Lakers players scored 20 or more points to lead them to a

114-100 win and their first ever championship in Los Angeles. After eight tries, the nightmare was finally over.

The champion Lakers made it back to the Finals in 1973 for a rematch with the Knicks. The Knicks easily won the series in five games. With the Finals loss the Lakers were coming to an end of dominance in the West. Chamberlain retired from the NBA after a legendary career, and West played his last season in 1974.

The Lakers played good ball throughout the 1970s but it wasn't enough to get them to the Finals. Kareem Abdul-Jabbar was the newest star for the Lakers. He was the league's Most Valuable Player (MVP) in both 1976 and 1977, but even Jabbar's awesome play at center couldn't win them a championship. It would take something magical to do that.

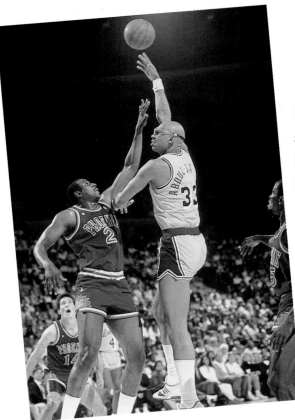

Kareem Abdul-Jabbar shoots his famous sky-hook over the head of a Phoenix Sun defender.

Los Angeles

George Mikan was the first superstar in the NBA. After the Lakers joined the NBA in 1948, Mikan led his team to five championships in six years.

Hall-of-Famer Elgin Baylor was named Rookie of the Year in the 1958-59 season.

After leading the Lakers to seven Western Conference Championships, Jerry West and the Lakers finally won the NBA Championship in the 1971-72 season.

Lakers

After leading the Lakers to an NBA
title in 1971-72, Wilt Chamberlain.
was named Finals MVP.

Magic Johnson led the
Lakers to five NBA
Championships in the
1980s. On his way he
picked up three
League MVPs and
three Finals MVPs.

Shaquille O'Neal was acquired by
the Lakers in 1996 to carry on the
great Laker tradition.

Magic Takes Over

For the 1979-80 season the Lakers added a player who was not only great but would turn the Laker franchise around. Earvin "Magic" Johnson was the first player picked in the NBA draft. The 6-foot, 9-inch Magic could play any position, but was at his best leading the team from the point.

Magic dazzled NBA audiences from coast to coast with a style of play that featured intelligent decision-making and unselfish distribution of the ball to his teammates.

Magic, along with Jabbar, who won his third MVP Award in five years, raced through the season and the playoffs to reach the NBA Finals for the first time in seven years.

In the Finals, the Lakers met the Philadelphia 76ers, who were led by Julius "Dr. J" Erving. The teams split the first two games in Los Angeles, and did the same in Philadelphia.

In Game 5, Jabbar injured his ankle in the third quarter, but came back to complete a 40-point performance in a 108-103 win. Because of his ankle, Jabbar was unable to play in Game 6, and the rookie sensation Magic Johnson played center for the Lakers, scoring 42 points and bringing down 15 rebounds for a Laker championship.

Magic was named the Finals MVP, with Jabbar coming in second. After an awesome rookie year, Magic was offered a 25-year, $25-million contract, the longest and richest in sports history to that point.

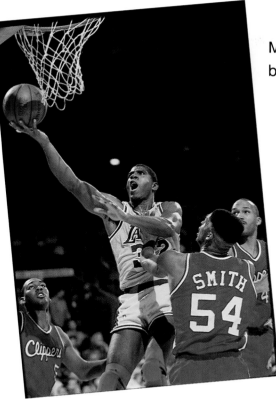

Magic Johnson drives the ball to the hoop.

Magic's contract, however, didn't guarantee Laker wins. He was injured the following season and played in only 37 games. The Lakers were ousted in the opening round of the playoffs.

In the 1982-83 season the Lakers got a new coach, and he installed a fast-break, run-and-gun offense. Pat Riley put his superstar Magic Johnson in charge of the new "Show-Time" offense. Show-Time worked to perfection, as the Lakers strolled through the playoffs to another Finals.

In the Finals the Lakers met the 76ers again. The Lakers won handily in six games, behind the play of Magic Johnson. In the final game, Magic scored 13 points with 13 rebounds and 13 assists. Again he was named Finals MVP.

The Lakers went to the Finals the following two seasons only to lose to the 76ers and the Boston Celtics. The loss to the Celtics would start one of the best rivalries in NBA history.

Magic Vs. Bird

In 1984, the NBA Finals matched the Boston Celtics against the Los Angeles Lakers. But everyone knew it was really Magic Johnson vs. Larry Bird. The Magic/Bird rivalry started back in college when Magic's Michigan State beat Bird's Indiana State in the NCAA Championship.

Magic Johnson leaps for joy in a victory over the Golden State Warriors.

Coming into the NBA, both Magic and Bird's teams looked for them to rebuild their franchises. They not only rebuilt their team, but they also took the NBA to a new level and made it one of the most popular professional sports in the world.

The rivalry continued in the 1985 Finals. The Lakers were playing in their eighth NBA Finals against the Celtics and had yet to beat them. Many believed the Lakers had the better team, but it didn't show in the first game as the Celtics embarrassed the Lakers 148-114. The recurring nightmare was coming back.

But the nightmare ended as the Lakers woke up and won four of the next five for the NBA Championship and an end to the jinx.

The Lakers were the odds-on favorite to repeat the following year. Before the season started, *Sports Illustrated* said the 1985-86 Laker team may have been the best NBA team ever assembled.

Early on they were right. The Lakers started with a 29-5 record and finished 62-20. It looked as though it would be Magic and Bird again, but the Lakers were ousted in the playoffs by the Houston Rockets, and the Celtics grabbed another title.

The following year it was Magic vs. Bird for the last time. And it ended in six games with Magic picking up the series MVP and the Lakers grabbing another title.

One of the greatest rivalries in professional sports had come to an end. The Magic/Bird rivalry was great because they were the best in the business. They both played hard, they both were team players, and they both made their teammates look good. The best aspect of the rivalry was that they respected each other and were good friends.

Magic said that Larry Bird was the only player that he feared. And Bird said that Magic was the greatest player he had ever played against. There will never be a rivalry like that of Magic and Bird.

Back-To-Back

Although the Celtics and Bird never made it back to the Finals, Magic and the Lakers did. The day after beating the Celtics, Coach Riley made a statement which aroused both surprise and criticism. He guaranteed a repeat championship.

Riley constantly repeated his statement and it worked. Behind one of the greatest line-ups in the history of the game, with Magic, Jabbar, A.C. Green, James Worthy, and Byron Scott, the Lakers easily made it to the Finals.

The Lakers met the "Bad Boys" of Detroit, who didn't want Riley's prediction to come true. The Pistons were led by Isiah Thomas, Bill Laimbeer, and Dennis Rodman.

It was a hard-fought series with the Pistons leading three to two after five games. In Game 6 it looked as though the Pistons had it won behind Isiah's 43 points, but the Lakers came back in the closing seconds to win 103-102.

In Game 7, Worthy took over for the Lakers. He had 36 points, 16 rebounds, and 10 assists to lead the Lakers to another title. For his brilliant play, he was awarded the series MVP.

Riley's guaranteed repeat came true, and the Lakers had their fifth title in nine years, easily giving them the distinction as the "Team of the '80s."

The Team Of The '80s Breaks Up

The 1988-89 season was to be Jabbar's 20th and last in the NBA. Another championship would have been a fitting sendoff for the 41-year old legend, but it wasn't to be. The Lakers were swept in the Finals by Detroit. Jabbar finished his illustrious career with the most points in the history of the game, with 38,387.

The following year, even without Jabbar, the Lakers won 63 regular season games. Magic was MVP in both the regular season and the All-Star Game, and Riley was named Coach of the Year.

The Lakers, though, were shocked in the playoffs, suffering an early-round defeat to the Phoenix Suns, four games to one. Soon afterward, Riley announced his resignation.

In the 1990-91 season, new coach Mike Dunleavy got the Lakers back to the Finals. This championship was known as Magic vs. Michael. Michael Jordan and the Chicago Bulls were in their first Finals.

It really wasn't much of a match-up, except for the first game, which the Lakers won. After that the Jordan-led Bulls dominated, winning four in a row, and capturing their first-ever NBA title.

For the Lakers it was their ninth NBA Finals in 12 years and their 24th overall. But to date it was their last.

Magic Says Good-Bye

On November 7, 1991, Magic announced his retirement because he had contracted HIV, which is responsible for AIDS. The fans still voted him into the All-Star Game, and with 25 points he was voted the MVP.

Staying in competitive shape, he would play again in public at the 1992 Olympic Games for the United States as part of the Dream Team. Magic, along with Bird, Jordan, and Charles Barkley, to name a few, would dominate all competition and win the gold medal.

Without Magic, the Lakers were never the same. He did make an attempt at a comeback but soon retired. He tried as head coach for the Lakers but didn't enjoy it. He tried once more as a player in 1996 but wasn't happy with the attitude of some of the younger players and retired again.

As for the Lakers' franchise, they have tried many different coaches and players since that last Finals appearance to get that winning combination. Coaches like Dunleavy, Randy Pfund, Magic, and Del Harris have all tried to lead the team.

Players like Vlade Divac, Elden Campbell, Sam Perkins, Cedric Ceballos, and Nick Van Excel are just a few who have tried from the court to get the Lakers back to the Finals. But there is one player that just might get them back.

Shaquille O'Neal slam dunks the ball for an easy two.

Lakers Hit The Shaqpot!

There was no way that one of the greatest franchises in the NBA was going to sit back and not make a move to improve the team. For the 1996-1997 season the Lakers made one of the biggest moves in NBA history.

The Lakers acquired one of the best centers and one of the most popular players in the game: Shaquille O'Neal. Acquiring O'Neal was an even bigger move than when they acquired either Chamberlain or Jabbar.

O'Neal was with the Orlando Magic for four years, where he literally built the team. After he became a free-agent, the Lakers signed him to the richest contract in NBA history. The 7-foot, 1-inch, 303-pound star center will be paid $121 million over seven years. But it won't be worth it unless he gets the Lakers back to the Finals and gets them a Championship.

In his first year with the Lakers, O'Neal turned the team around. The Lakers became the hottest ticket in the NBA. After winning 56 games the Lakers dominated the Portland Trail Blazers in the first round of the playoffs. In the second round they were matched against the eventual Western Conference Champions, Utah Jazz. The Jazz, however, were too much for the Lakers, easily taking the series in five games.

Shaq didn't get the Lakers to the NBA Finals, but it shouldn't be long before he does. The Lakers have a young and talented team. Besides Shaq, the team also has 18-year-old Kobe Bryant, forwards Elden Campbell and Robert Horry, and guard Eddie Jones, to a name a few of the talented youngsters.

The Lakers franchise has been in the Finals a record 24 times and has been NBA Champions 11 times, second only to the Boston Celtics. A franchise like the Lakers cannot stay down too long. And when they bring in a player like Shaquille O'Neal, it is only a matter of time before they are champions again.

Elden Campbell blocks a shot by the Portland Trail Blazers' Clifford Robinson.

Glossary

American Basketball Association (ABA)—A professional basketball league that rivaled the NBA from 1967 to 1976 until it merged with the NBA.

assist—A pass of the ball to the teammate scoring a field goal.

Basketball Association of America (BAA)—A professional basketball league that merged with the NBL to form the NBA.

center—A player who holds the middle position on the court.

championship—The final basketball game or series, to determine the best team.

draft—An event held where NBA teams choose amateur players to be on their team.

expansion team—A newly-formed team that joins an already established league.

fast break—A play that develops quickly down court after a defensive rebound.

field goal—When a player scores two or three points with one shot.

Finals—The championship series of the NBA playoffs.

forward—A player who is part of the front line of offense and defense.

franchise—A team that belongs to an organized league.

free throw—A privilege given a player to score one point by an unhindered throw for goal from within the free-throw circle and behind the free-throw line.

guard—Either of two players who initiate plays from the center of the court.

jump ball—To put the ball in play in the center restraining circle with a jump between two opponents at the beginning of the game, each extra period, or when two opposing players each have control of the ball.

Most Valuable Player (MVP) Award—An award given to the best player in the league, All-Star Game, or NBA Finals.

National Basketball Association (NBA)—A professional basketball league in the United States and Canada, consisting of the Eastern and Western conferences.

National Basketball League (NBL)—A professional basketball league that merged with the BAA to form the NBA.

National Collegiate Athletic Association (NCAA)—The ruling body which oversees all athletic competition at the college level.

personal foul—A player foul which involves contact with an opponent while the ball is alive or after the ball is in the possession of a player for a throw-in.

playoffs—Games played by the best teams after the regular season to determine a champion.

postseason—All the games after the regular season ends; the playoffs.

rebound—To grab and control the ball after a missed shot.

rookie—A first-year player.

Rookie of the Year Award—An award given to the best first-year player in the league.

Sixth Man Award—An award given yearly by the NBA to the best non-starting player.

trade—To exchange a player or players with another team.

Index